The Appalachian Way in Coal Country

LOIS WALKER WEST

ISBN 978-1-64258-811-8 (paperback)
ISBN 978-1-64416-510-2 (hardcover)
ISBN 978-1-64258-812-5 (digital)

Christian Faith Publishing, Inc.
832 Park Avenue
Meadville, PA 16335
www.christianfaithpublishing.com

Printed in the United States of America

I dedicate my story to my wonderful sisters and thank them for assisting me with their memories. And, to all the families that once lived in the Allais, Kentucky, mining camp near Hazard.

In Loving Memory of my Dad, Mom and brother David

Jerry Walker (Dad)

David Lawrence Walker and Mom
(Sibyl Walker)

Old Family Photo taken by David L. Walker

Geraldine, Billie, Joyce, Doris, Lois, Mom and Dad

Contents

Introduction

Kentucky—the land of "fast horses and pretty women," or is it "pretty horses and fast women." I guess it depends on who's telling the story. You may have to look a long time to find very many fast horses in Eastern Kentucky, but pretty women are there to be found. Some people think if you were born in Eastern Kentucky you lived a life of poverty with one dress made from a chicken feed sack and no shoes and lived off welfare with very little food. We have been called hillbillies, briar-hoppers, hicks from the hills, and heaven only knows what else. I can only speak for myself by saying that I am very proud to be from Kentucky and a coalminer's daughter. I treasure all my memories of the past, and every now and then that one very exciting moment from the past comes out in a conversation with my children and grandchildren. I want them to know and seek out their heritage. It wasn't very often that I took the opportunity to visit the place where I grew up. The place that molded me into the person I am today. I can't imagine in this day having to live in the hills of Kentucky in a small house on a hillside with no electricity, water, or indoor plumbing. We had no indoor bathroom, phone, TV, refrigerator, or air conditioner. But crazy as it sounds, when I was a child, I loved that place! Did I just say that?? Maybe I just don't remember being unhappy living there. I was born in 1938 along with a twin sister in Allais, a coal mining area near Hazard, Kentucky. Mom had now given birth to six children, one boy and five girls—the twins being the youngest and the boy the oldest. When the babies started coming two at a time, Dad was convinced the family was big enough. We were all raised with very strict morals and values. Southeastern Kentucky, was known as a poverty-stricken area to outsiders. But I don't ever remember going hungry, and if we were poor, I didn't know it! We may have been, but now I feel I was blessed with a wealth of information as I grew up in that Appalachian area. Living in the city now, I miss the mountains, the fresh spring water we drank, and the homegrown meats and vegetables. How much more "organic" could we be? Every visit I made to Allais, Kentucky, brought back many wonderful memories. This once booming coal mining community was a place where I felt safe as I walked to and from school and enjoyed a playground of twenty-plus acres around my family's home in the mountains of Eastern Kentucky.

1

Where in the Heck Is Allais?!

I left early one morning and drove south from Middletown, Ohio, to visit Allais, Kentucky. I don't know why I decided to take Interstate 75 that day. I hated busy highways. I felt as though I was in a rat's race in the middle of several lanes of traffic. The joy of my trip was already in question knowing I was taking my life in my hands every time I dared to look sideways! Not too many people nowadays enjoy traveling the scenic routes. Time today is evidently more important than looking at something beautiful along the old highways. In the early 1950s, driving from Ohio to Allais on the old two-lane routes took more than eight hours of almost enjoyable driving through the mountains of Kentucky. The numerous curves up and down the mountains could make even the strongest stomach sick, especially if you were riding in the backseat. Today the trip only takes about five hours. The new roads are great, but how can you see the real country while you're flying down the highway and going seventy miles an hour? I doubt if the old moonshine runners had any problems driving on the winding roads. Many years ago bootlegging liquor or "white lightning" as it was called was one way of making money. It wasn't too hard for the bootleggers to hide all the equipment needed to make the white lightning in the densely wooded hills. I believe some of my relatives were even involved at one time. Maybe not for profit, but a little homemade brew for personal use was always a good thing for many of the men living in the mountainous region. But my mother hated everything about it! It's strange the things you remember when you go back to your old home place.

The last stretch of the new highway cut through the tops of the mountains and took away the beautiful view we had from my family's front porch. I was completely surprised when I took the exit leading into Allais and Hazard. I felt lost for a minute as I glanced around the area trying to recognize exactly where I was. This had to be Walkertown where I went to grade school. Walkertown (named after my great grandfather) was only minutes from Allais. When I left Kentucky in 1956, the paved road ended at the commissary and post office in Allais. Walkertown seemed so far away when my sisters and I walked to and from school.

Where in the heck is Allais? It was on the map when I lived here! My mailing address was simply Allais, Kentucky. The post office of Allais as I knew it long ago doesn't exist anymore! The postmaster was very friendly as he greeted everyone by name when handing them their mail. Sometimes he would kiddingly ask me, "What's your name, little girl?" I was better known then as one of the "little Walker twins." Glancing around the area I wanted to get out of my car and walk the familiar road once again. But would anyone even recognize me? I'm not sure what year Allais dropped off the map, but it still existed in 1956, the year I graduated from Hazard High. Part of the area was like walking back in time and sparking bits and pieces of the past. The sidewalk leading up to the grade school was the same, and the many small, familiar business buildings were still standing along the road. At the corner gas station, the road divided as it entered the Allais area. What a thrill it was to spend that last nickel I had saved from my lunch money to buy a Payday or Three Musketeers candy bar as I walked home from grade school. This was also the gathering place where the older kids caught the school bus going to Hazard High. If anyone was late arriving at the bus stop, it was just too bad; you then had to find your own way to school or walk back home. I wonder how many kids were sometimes deliberately late.

2

The Birth of Allais

David's First Job in Allais Mining Camp

by Lois Walker West

I n 1750, Thomas Walker, an explorer, discovered coal in Eastern Kentucky. He was the first to burn coal in a campfire in the woods. Whether or not he is an ancestor, I don't know, but I would like to think he was. I do know that my ancestors were among the first pioneers that settled in the coal-rich southeastern area of Kentucky in the early 1800s. These mountains were once known as the Walker Mountains. At one time, my great-great-grandfather John (1814–1898) was a judge of Perry county and owned thousands of acres in Hazard and the adjoining community of Allais and Walkertown (named after the Walkers). From the information I now have, John K. Walker was a very prosperous man. I was surprised when I found out that he donated the land to build the Petrey Memorial Baptist church that our family attended while living in Allais.

When my great-grandfather, Jeremiah "Jerry Pete" Walker, found out his land was rich with coal, he leased a large part of his land along with the mineral rights to the Columbus Mining Company. The mining lease that was in effect when I grew up in Allais was issued in 1925 and ended in 1954. The company during that time employed approximately 151 miners. He also sold or gave the right-of way for the first railroad in the area to the Louisville and Nashville R.R. Co. The railroad tracks were laid all the way to the coal mines. Many tons of coal were taken out of the mountains in railroad cars, each filled until they were running over. The lonesome sounds of train whistles could be heard for miles as the trains made their way to and from the mine. Operations of the mine did not always run smoothly. After the union was voted in, the employees would sometimes go on strike to settle safety issues and wage disagreements. This resulted in many hardships for the miners and their families. Where the coal from this mine was delivered to, I don't know!

This coal mining community was named Allais and was located near the north fork of the Kentucky River, which was known to flood many times. I never really thought about how Allais became the name of this community until I looked up the census for 1940. There I found that the name "Allais" was actually the last name of one of the supervisors of the coal mine. Allais was now on the official map of Kentucky with its own post office. The opening of the coal mine created many jobs. As word spread about the opening of a new coal mine, men and their families began moving to the area for work. Carpenters as well as coal miners were needed. Large two-story boarding houses and hundreds of smaller homes had to be built to accommodate the miners and their families. Soon the hillsides were dotted with "camp houses." From the moment one entered Allais, you knew you were in a coal mining community. A maze of narrow dirt roads winding through the coal mining area created what we now call "subdivisions." Some houses were built so close together you could talk to one another from your front porch. Others were built on such a steep hillside it was surprising the foundations didn't collapse from the dirt washing away underneath them. But some people may have enjoyed living on the steep hillsides. At least they had a better view of the area. When many workers started moving into this area, they were probably lucky to find an empty house.

The worst place where several two-story houses stood was in an area we called "the hole" and in the flood zone.

When the floods came, it was so scary to see water covering the lower half of all the houses. Seeing this really made me appreciate our house on the hillside. The only good thing I remember about the area was the baseball field the community made. One large flat and sandy area lay closer to the river's edge and was perfect for the field. Many young men in the area loved playing baseball. On game day you could see fans standing along the paved road leading into Allais where one could look down upon the ball field and watch the game. There's nothing any better than free entertainment!

Allais became a large, fast-growing area and soon became a thriving coal mining community. A commissary, which housed the post office and other offices needed by the supervisors of the mine, was built. This made it very convenient for all the miners living in the area. The commissary sold just about everything a family needed, including groceries, clothing, and many other household items. Miners were allowed to charge their groceries and have it deducted from their payroll checks. Sometimes these charges would amount to almost all their checks. Families had to live and manage with what they earned. My father earned very little in the year 1943 as a coal miner. The land he owned and farmed helped our family survive. As a child, I always wondered why my friends living nearby thought we were wealthy. Looking back, I now realize why they felt that way. Our family was a landowner in the area and even though Dad worked for the Columbus Mining Company, he was still the grandson of the man who leased his land to start the coal mining community.

During all my childhood years, I knew nothing about my family's ancestors. My parents never discussed any family history. I was married with a family of my own before I ever asked any specific questions regarding my grandparents. Grandma Walker had died the year I was born, and thus, all my sisters and I were denied the love of a grandmother. Grandpa John Walker lived with Aunt Grace, dad's sister, during his last years. I only knew him as an elderly, white-haired man who sat on my aunt's porch most of the time, watching the people as they passed by. I saw him there many times as I walked to school. I realized now that I never carried on a conversation with my grandfather. Why didn't I take the time to stop and talk to him? He feels like a stranger from the past.

I knew most of my dad's immediate family, but he never talked about how he inherited the land for our first home from his father. This was a large parcel of land at the end of the hollow. The land where our second house stood once belonged to Uncle Joe Walker, my father's brother. Dad purchased Uncle Joe's land in 1939 after he sold his first property.

3

What's a Holler?

I can always start an interesting conversation when I tell someone I was born in a "holler," or hollow. My oldest sister's husband from Ohio enjoyed telling everyone that when we were old enough, we had to swing out on a grapevine. It's a good thing her vine didn't break. Another old tale was we lived so far back in the hills the sunshine had to be piped in. I never did find those pipes!

Well, our little hollow had its good points! Parents could walk out on their porches and shout out to the neighbors or their kids and get a response in minutes. No one needed a phone! The communication was all free! Everyone knew when someone's child was not home at dusk, and you knew their name as it echoed through the valley. But how embarrassing it was when suddenly you heard *your* name and the final announcement was, "YOU BETTER GET HOME RIGHT THIS MINUTE!"

The large coal mine nearby where my father spent many years working was up another hollow called Walker's

Branch, but some people called it "Niger Hollow" (no offense intended). This was also the only African-American community nearby during those days of segregation. The kids attended their own schools and churches. I wasn't aware or old enough then to question why it was this way. I did think it was strange they always walked to the back when riding the city bus. I also thought maybe they just wanted to sit in the back like the kids on the school bus. They fought over the backseat. I'm so glad they finally stood up for their rights. Bad things in the world were not discussed by my parents. Those issues were not something a child could solve. We lived in our own little "holler." I don't remember ever talking to an African-American person until later in life when I lived in Ohio and had my first full-time job.

Even though the area we lived in was Allais, many people knew one another by the hollow you lived in. Every hollow had its own name. The hollow where my family lived was called the Holiness Hollow, most likely named because many families living there attended the Holiness Church across the river. I'm not sure if that was the proper name or not.

Driving into these hollows on narrow dirt roads could be an experience in itself. Every time I revisited my hollow, I found it difficult to visualize where all the many camp houses once stood. During my visits, I was amazed to see some of the original camp-built houses still lining each side of the road. Most of the houses had a new coat of paint with flowers blooming in the small yards. After the closing of the coal mine, many of these homes were put up for sale and bought by their renters. At the bend of the road, one still had to drive through the shallow creek water. Most of the year, the creek was very calm, with cold water making soft rippling sounds over the small pebbles. But after a heavy rainstorm, the water became very muddy as it rushed quickly down the valleys between each hillside. The more it rained, the bigger and wider the streams became. Sometimes the water would almost cover the small wooden bridges and walkways everyone used to cross the creek. Very few families here were fortunate enough to own a car, so walking or riding the city bus was the only way to their destination.

Walking in and out of the hollow seemed like miles as a child, but now I can say it was only a "hop and a jump." Standing at the foot of the hill, looking up toward the only flat area on the hillside where "the big white house" (as we called it) stood made me very sad. My happy childhood days were gone. The twenty or more camp houses that stood on each side of the dirt road in the upper part of the hollow were also gone. The huge slate dump, created by the coal mining company as the coal was separated from the slate, was once alive with the laughter and the noise of many kids playing games. Now it's covered over with trees and shrubs. The mountains have slowly reclaimed their original appearance. Is this what my great-grandfather saw when he first leased this land to the mining company? The realization of how quickly things change makes me feel very fortunate. This land may not be in the family forever, but I still have something that I can pass on to my generation: my wonderful memories of the years I grew up in this "holler"—memories that keep us all tied together.

4

The Big White House

"The Big White House" by Lois Walker West

The big white house on the hill is no longer there, but I can still see it sitting high on the hill. Compared to the three- or four-room camp houses, our white house was rather nice—even without all the conveniences of today. It wasn't by any means a *big* house, but the white paint made it stand out above all the other dull brown unpainted houses in the coal mining camp. It sat over-looking the hollow like a watch dog. We had a view that would make anyone envious. Every day or so, we could see the train in the far distance making its way through the mountains to pick up the coal. My twin sister and I would sometimes sit on the porch steps and count the number of rail cars the train would be pulling as we watched for the bright red caboose. The small dirt path, which was a short cut around the hill leading into our hollow, was also visible. Most everyone in the hollow used the short-cut, thus mak-ing it possible for us to see everyone coming and going. There were no surprise visitors to our house.

Besides being a coal miner, Dad could do about any kind of carpenter work. The large porch he added across the front of the house was a favorite place to play, espe-cially on rainy days. That old swing on the front porch really took a beating. We always had to see just how high we could push one another. Sometimes the chains holding the swing to the ceiling could not hold all the weight of three or four kids and one side would break. With a terri-ble jolt down we would go crashing to the floor screaming as we fell. Mom would come running out the door to see if we were okay. There were a few bruises every now and then but no broken bones. Our favorite game was fruit basket turnover. Each child was named a different fruit. Then everyone sat in a circle with one person in the mid-dle. The one in the middle called out the names of two fruits to change places. As the two scrambled for a newly vacated chair, the caller had to quickly grab an open seat. If he wasn't successful after several calls, he then called out "fruit basket turn over," and everyone had to change chairs. Hopefully that caller found a chair open and someone else was left standing.

As our family grew, Dad added more rooms to our original three-room house. We now had a living room, dining room, and kitchen, plus two bedrooms with an attic for another bedroom. All five girls reluctantly or lovingly shared one bedroom. Two double-size beds and one dresser was all that would fit in the small room with a fireplace. The only closet in our bedroom was also used for all the home canned food. A yummy jar of home canned peaches was known to disappear late at night from time to time. At least it was a healthy snack!

The one large attic room where my brother slept (the oldest child) was partially complete. I'm sure he enjoyed his privacy and was glad to get as far away as possible from five girls. To keep us pesky girls out of his room, he stuck straight pins in the top step of the stairway. That was mean, but it worked! It definitely was enough convincing to keep me out of his room!

Dad never stopped working around the house. He felt the chickens needed a house, so he built a chicken house in the back yard with lots of places for them to lay eggs. But, it was strange the chickens would not sleep in the chicken house. They always flew up in a large tree and slept there over night. Then in the front yard he built a small shed to cover the coal and keep it dry. After a large truck delivered the coal and dumped it at the bottom of the hill, everyone in the family took turns carrying the coal up the hill. Sometimes it took several days to get this done. But, if you went down the hill, you better come back up with a lump of coal!

5

The Outhouse

Our outhouse was just another name for what is now a bathroom. We couldn't call ours a bathroom since it was never used as a place to take a bath. Our outhouse facility was an outdoor toilet located just far enough away but only a short distance from the house. Every house in the mining camp had one. Some families even built one with two holes to sit on. I don't believe there was any reading in these outhouses! It would have been a little difficult to hold your nose and turn the pages in a book. The smell was enough to make you exit very quickly even with all the open-air spaces in the walls.

When the hole in our little outhouse was full, Dad simply dug another and moved the small building over the new one. The short walk to the outhouse in the middle of the night, especially with no moon shining, was very scary. The flashlight we carried was no comfort at all. But, we all felt safer when Dad carried the flashlight and walked with us. We always imagined some wild animal jumping out of the woods and killing us, especially after we found our puppy on the porch ripped to pieces by a wild cat one day after school.

Our toilet tissue had a lot to be desired, but one could catch up with the latest styles thumbing through the Sears and Montgomery Ward catalogues looking for a soft sheet of paper. Our wish books now became our *wipe* books. No one wanted to use the colored pages—you see, they were just too *slick*! I suppose Mom couldn't justify spending money on toilet tissue.

It was in our little outhouse that my oldest sister, at the age of thirteen, discovered she needed glasses. While peering through the cracks in the walls, she noticed a difference in the vision of each eye. A trip to the eye doctor corrected that with a dreadful pair of eye glasses. No one wanted to be called four-eyes!

One summer, Uncle Joe came to visit us from Ohio and brought his small daughter. I thought it was very funny when Linda remarked, "What a cute little house," when we showed her our *bathroom*. Knowing we were having company, we had put forth a little extra effort to make our outhouse as clean as possible. Brushing away the cobwebs full of insects helped somewhat, but there was very little we could do about the smell. Even though Dad kept lye poured in the hole to keep the odor down, no one had to worry about anyone occupying the outhouse very long. When Linda asked my twin sister and me to leave her alone to use the bathroom, we were afraid that she might fall in the hole, so we offered her our help. When she insisted "No help wanted," we watched through the cracks in the wall to make sure she was okay. She didn't stay inside very long. I don't believe she thought our outhouse was a "cute little house," anymore and she quickly told us that our toilet tissue was terrible.

6

Howdy, Neighbor

It doesn't matter where you live; neighbors come and go during your life span. Some you may want to forget, but others will be remembered for a very long time. Babysitting with the neighbors' little ones, helping my favorite friend with chores so she could come out and play, flirting with the boy next door, or just taking a walk in the woods helped create the memories I can't forget. Families actually knew one another by name, and everyone always greeted each other with a loud, "Howdy." Our neighbors were hardworking, law-abiding families living a simple life. Neighbors can be great people. I've found that from Kentucky to Ohio and now Florida.

During my childhood years in Allais, I played outside and had fun with many friends most of the year. Yes, there were some fights or disagreements among the kids, but those didn't last long. There was never a problem in finding enough kids to play a ball game at any time. The open lot in the middle of the hollow where once sat a two-story house made the perfect ball field. The house had burned to the ground and was never rebuilt. It was a terrible day, but neighbors helped water down the houses nearby to keep them safe.

For many families in the mining camp, most of the rooms in their small houses except the kitchen were used as bedrooms. The large porches served as their living room and provided an excellent place to entertain neighbors and catch up with the latest gossip while doing some daily chores. My love of craft making came from watching several women in the neighborhood making beautiful crepe paper flowers for Memorial Day, or Decoration Day as we knew it then. Small flower pedals were cut out and then stretched and twisted to form roses and other beautiful flowers in many different colors. This is probably one of the many lost arts from the past. The work and love they put into these bouquets of flowers were taken to the cemetery to decorate the graves of their loved ones.

Many times you could see the neighborhood mothers ironing clothes on their porches during the hot summer months. Believe it or not, every item of clothing everyone owned was made from 100 percent cotton. There was no such thing as wash-and-wear fabric. The old irons Mom used were kept hot on the kitchen stove as she did her ironing. This chore required two irons, one to leave on the stove and stay hot and the other to iron with. Switching was done with interchangeable handles. If you look carefully, you may find these irons today in your local antique shop. Some people use them as book ends.

The man in the long black coat living in our neighborhood was a mystery to all the little kids in the mining camp. Every evening at about the same time, anyone could see him walking home from work wearing his long black coat. Then suddenly one day, Mom wanted my twin sister and me to take our worn-out shoes and have this man put new soles on them. We didn't want to go, but Mom insisted he was a good man and knew how to fix shoes very well. She handed us some money and our old shoes. Slowly we walked down the hill and up the creek to his three-room house. We only had to knock once. The door opened slowly as we stood there with our shoes in our hands, looking up at this tall dirty-looking man. We stumbled with our words as we told him what we wanted. Then he asks us if we wanted to come in while he worked on our shoes. We both stayed close to each other as we stepped inside the front door. It was extremely dark inside with all the curtains closed. Stacks of old newspapers and books lined every wall. He cleared a chair for us to sit on and pulled out a shoe stand and tools to fix our shoes. We watched as he took off the old soles and cut a new piece of leather to nail on the bottom of each shoe. When he was finished, he handed us back our shoes and ask very slowly, "Are you Jerry's twins?"

"Yes," we replied and handed him the money Mom had given us to pay him. This was one time we really wanted new shoes after we looked at the shiny ugly nails on the bottom of them. Many years later, I found out that this man was very intelligent and was the one who kept all the records for the miners' union.

7

Raised the Organic Way

You can't go to the supermarkets today without seeing items marked "organic." The word *organic* was never used when I was a child. It meant absolutely nothing to our family or anyone else in the neighborhood. I now realize how fortunate we were to have grown up in an area where mostly all of the food we ate was homegrown. Mom never asked anyone what they wanted for dinner or any other meal. If she had, she probably would have received more requests than she wanted. I loved the food we ate without realizing how healthy it was for the family. There were many times I wanted the store-bought items such as "light" bread (this is a loaf of white bread) and the boxed cereals you didn't have to cook. We never bought bottled milk from the grocery store. We drank raw milk fresh from the neighbor's cow. It wasn't pasteurized or homogenized. The cream was visible on top of the milk, and Mom shook the bottle well to mix the milk before we could drink it. If the milk became sour before it was all drank, it was never thrown away. The old churn was then pulled out of the cupboard, and after several hours of taking turns churning the sour milk, we had delicious homemade butter. Mom would carefully spoon the soft fluffy butter off the top of the churned milk and whip it with a fork until it was nice and thick. The remaining milk was thicker and was one of our favorite drinks. It was now homemade buttermilk. Mom only owned a cow for a short time. Milking it every day was more work than she could handle. One of Dad's favorite snacks was the homemade butter mashed up together with hot cornbread. I would rather have my cornbread broke into pieces and put in a glass of milk and eaten with a spoon.

Our naturally purified water came from an underground mountain stream. To keep the water as clean as possible, Dad built a small house from lime rock he chiseled out of the mountains to cover the holding pool. We called it our springhouse. The door to the springhouse was no more than four feet high, which made it a little difficult to get inside. A dipper made from a dried gourd we grew in the garden was kept in the springhouse to dip water from the holding pool into our bucket. Another gourd was kept in the bucket to drink from. Everyone drank from the same dipper, and no one ever thought about getting someone else's germs. The springhouse also provided a convenient place to keep perishable food cool. My sisters and I all hated going inside because bugs and spiders and other creepy animals found the damp, cool house a cozy place to live in. A flashlight came in handy to check the inside of the dark springhouse. Once inside we wasted no time in filling the bucket with water. Carrying the bucket back to the house was no problem for my twin and me as we both held the handle between us. The real problem was keeping the water in it. By the time we reached the house, our legs were wet from the water splashing out of the bucket. Families living in the camp houses had their own supply of water. Several hand pumps from wells were located throughout the mining camp, which conveniently provided the families with water.

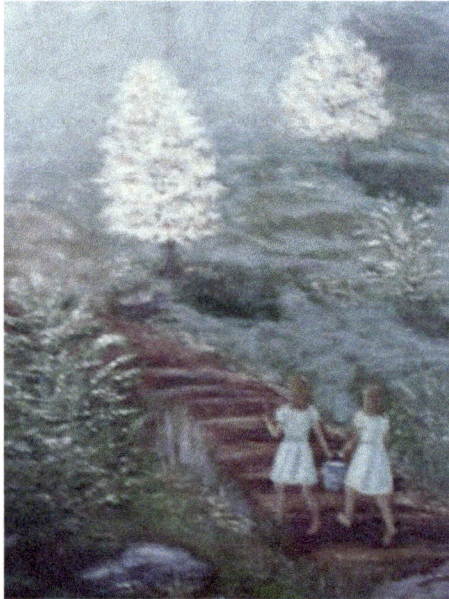

"Water From the Mountain Spring"
by Lois Walker West
My twin and I carrying water
from our mountain spring.

Our family lived mostly off the abundance of our land. The rich soil produced all the vegetables we needed to feed our family for the many years we lived there. But gardening wasn't easy work. Everyone had to do their share. Together the family spent many hours from early spring to late fall planting and harvesting fruits and vegetables. Just preparing the garden area for planting was a huge chore. Dad had to hire a neighbor with a horse to plow and till the soil for our garden. Since the property where our house stood only had one small flat area at the bottom of the hill, this had to be a tedious task just guiding the horse and plow through the garden. I don't know how that horse kept from stumbling and falling down the steep hillside. Now don't believe the old tale that the horses and cows in Kentucky have two short legs from walking on the steep hillsides. I know for a fact this isn't true. They kept them all the same size by walking different directions—believe it or not!

Sometimes a nearby family needed space for a garden. If at all possible, Dad would find a plot for them to grow the vegetables they needed. Neighbors were always willing to work together. I believe people today have forgotten those work habits. Since there was only one boy in our family, the girls worked just as hard as boys. After the garden area was all plowed and tilled to a fine, loose soil, my twin sister and I loved to start at the top of the hill and run all the way to the bottom in our bare feet; but our playground only lasted a short time. Once Dad cleaned out the chicken house and the manure was spread all over the garden for fertilizer, we no longer found it fun. How could something that smells so bad make vegetables grow so big and taste so good? Soon we were put to work dropping kernels of corn, beans, and other seeds. The worst part of planting the garden was carrying buckets of water from the spring to water the tomato, cabbage, and sweet potato plants. Even though it was only a short distance, it seemed like miles away. We always started with a full bucket of water from the spring. But after we walked up the bank from the spring, passed the house and the outhouse, went down through the gully and over another creek and up the bank to the garden, we were lucky if we had *any* water left in the bucket. Are you thinking we should have used a water hose? Well, our little spring had no water faucet to connect to, and I don't remember ever seeing a water hose back then!

As the plants began to grow, so did the weeds. It took lots of hoeing in order to keep the weeds out of the garden. The rows were so long we found ourselves sitting down to rest at the end of each one. No one enjoyed this job, but come fall we were all rewarded with the taste of fresh vegetables. There's nothing like a fresh red tomato just off the vine. Every vegetable that wasn't used in the summer was canned or stored away for the winter months. Organic gardening was nothing new to us; it was just plain hard work!

Mom had the seemingly never ending task of canning all those organic, homegrown vegetables, and we were not excluded from helping. Corn had to be shucked and cut off the cob. The skins were removed from tomatoes after being dipped in hot water, and the cabbage was chopped to make sauerkraut and relishes. All this was done without the use of any electrical appliances. Dad made a perfect chopper from a tin can by taking the cap off one end. Holding the uncut end, Mom could chop up a dishpan full of raw vegetables to make the relish in a very short time. When this chopper became dull, Dad just threw it away and made another one. Bushels full of white half-runner beans were broken into pieces after the strings were removed. Sometimes we would get an assembly line going with one person stringing and another breaking the beans. The only fun part was using a needle and thread to string the unbroken beans together like popcorn in order to hang them up to dry. When dry, these were called shuckie beans. I've yet to figure out how they got this name.

Mom saved her canning jars from year to year, and the dusty jars had to be carefully washed in hot soapy water. The kids with the smallest hands were elected to wash the insides of the jars. My twin and I seemed to always get this job. After the jars were packed and sealed, Mom placed them in a large cooker on top of the stove or in the big black pot in our backyard that sat over an open fire. This finished the canning process. It was several years before Mom could afford a pressure cooker, which would have saved her many hours of work. But I don't think she ever felt safe using it. She was always afraid this cooker would blow up, especially when it started hissing and steaming out of the little knob that sat on the top of the pot. This was a warning to turn the heat down, but how do you turn the heat down on an old wood-burning stove? Just move the pot to a cooler part of the stove!

Most of the fruits Mom canned came from peddlers. Large trucks loaded with fresh produce arrived in the hollow during the summer months. The driver's voice echoed loudly as he announced the produce he was peddling, such as "Apples! Peaches!" The echo of his voice left no one unaware of his arrival. In a matter of minutes, several women would be gathered around the large truck waiting their turn to buy the fresh fruits or vegetables. The best fruit ever was the juicy freestone peaches. Sometimes Mom would let us eat all we wanted, but she also knew when it was enough. Her remark then was "We won't have anything to can if you keep eating"! That was sometimes hard to do with the smell of the fresh fruit and the juices running down our arms as we peeled the peaches. All the other work was put on hold until the canning was completed. Our neighbor had no qualms about asking for help if Mom no longer needed us. Most of her children at that time were all too young to help.

Cherries were the only fruit Mom canned from trees on our land. The large red cherry tree stood just outside the kitchen door. Who needed a boy to climb that tree? Mom always caught us sitting in the tree eating the ripe juicy fruit. She then just handed us a pail and said, "Pick me enough for a pie while you're up there!" The cherry cobblers Mom made were quite delicious, but I was really surprised when

I ate a pie someone else had made and it contained no pits! Who had time to remove pits? Not Mom!

Blackberry picking was a day's job. The bugs loved us as we made our way up the hill through the tall weeds in search of the berries. My sisters and I all had our own pail. The wild blackberries grew on the hillsides at the back of our house. Sometimes we would remember exactly where to find them from the previous year. But so did everyone else in the neighborhood. If we were lucky, we were the first ones to the patch, but watch out for the snakes! Everyone's goal was to make it back home with a full pail of berries. My twin sister and I just wanted enough to make a delicious treat with a glass full of sweet berries covered with milk and a little sugar! That was just about as good as Mom's home-made blackberry cobbler!

All too soon, summer was over. The hard work of canning vegetables was done. The only vegetables left in the garden were the potatoes. These had to be dug at the right time and after the vines had all died. Dad took great care in digging the potatoes and made sure there were no cuts on each one. To keep them through the winter months, Dad would dig a large shallow hole near the house and line it with burlap bags. This kept the potatoes from freezing during the coldest winter months. The potatoes were then placed in the hole and covered with more burlap bags. When the winter months arrived and Mom needed some potatoes to cook, it was a little more difficult to find someone who was willing to go outside and dig the potatoes from the hole. We were always glad when Dad was home and took over that chore. It was no fun going outside without gloves when it was below freezing and scrapping away frozen dirt on top of burlap bags while kneeling down in the snow. It was a lot harder than opening a cupboard door in a warm kitchen! I have to admit though—the taste of those potatoes made it all worth the work. Today if someone asks me, "Why are you so healthy"? I can only reply, "Because I was raised the organic way."

8

Surviving the Great Depression

My mom and dad lived and survived during some of the most difficult times of our country. The talents they possessed to do this could not have been better with a college degree. Dad was not only a coal miner but also a carpenter, stone cutter, farmer, butcher, and hunter, and he had a lot of common sense. He cleared the land that was given to him by his father. And with the help of his brother, he built the first house that he and my mother owned. During the Great Depression years, they had four children; and at the end of that era, they had twins. My mother was a great cook, seamstress, and wonderful mother to six children. Cleanliness to her was as the old saying goes: "Next to godliness."

Even during the hardest of times, Dad made sure we had enough coal to heat the house during the winter months. He knew there was still coal in the abandoned mine at the bottom of the hill. If needed he and a friend would dig the coal and haul it out with a small pony pulling a cart.

During my years in Kentucky, I don't ever remember going hungry. Thanks for the knowledge and the ability my Mom and Dad possessed to farm and preserve food.

9

Surviving with War Ration Stamps

I'm sure there were times when every family in the coal mining community felt the pressure of providing the needs of their children. During the time of World War II, the government felt it necessary to issue ration stamps on certain items. My twin sister and I were only four years old when the first book of stamps was issued in 1942. The next three issues were in January, October, and in late 1943. Every member in a family was eligible to receive a book of stamps. The books and stamps inside were all numbered and came with a list of very strict instructions. Any retail store had to accept these stamps. When one needed to buy an item that was rationed, a stamp had to be used along with the payment. Stamps could not be transferred to another individual. Violation of the rules could be a fine as high as ten thousand dollars. The retail clerk had to remove the stamp from your book when you bought one of the items. I cannot name every item that was rationed, but sugar, coffee, and shoes were three that Mom used. Mom could always replace the sugar with molasses, but nothing replaced the shoes we needed. This had to be the reason she impressed on each of us to take care of them. She always insisted that we wear an old pair when playing at home.

I can still hear Mom calling after Dot, my older sister, "Don't run! You'll tear the shoes off your feet!" Although we knew how Mom felt, my twin and I were still too proud to wear ugly boots over our shoes even when the rainy months made the dirt road through the hollow a pathway of mud. As careful as we were, we found it very difficult to find a rock big enough to step on or a dry spot where we could keep the mud off our shoes. At times we would lose our balance and find ourselves stepping into a pool of wet mud. Our sister Gerri was a little smarter than we were. She would wear an old pair of shoes through the mud and carry her good ones. Once we reached the paved road all she had to do was switch shoes. She was very particular in how she looked, even in grade school.

Staples such as sugar, cornmeal, flour, and pinto beans (soup beans) were bought at the miners' commissary. The pinto beans helped us survive the winter months. I still love soup beans served with hot cornbread! Mom would send whichever child was around to the commissary with a list of items she needed. We loved any excuse to go out of the hollow to the store. Since Joyce and I were so shy, the clerk found it much easier to take our list and find the items himself. He then put them in a paper poke (this is a brown paper bag). The candy behind the counter tempted us as we waited for the list to be filled. But we never dared buy anything extra—not even a dope. If you don't know what a dope is, it's a bottle of Coca-Cola or any other flavored soda.

Mom never bought anything she didn't need. She would make do with whatever was in the house, like making gravy with cornmeal instead of flour. It tasted pretty good, and we thought it was just another one of her good recipes until she told Dot later that she used cornmeal because she was out of flour. Sometimes for a little extra flavor, she added a little chopped green onion.

Another much needed staple was molasses. Mom never lost her taste for molasses through the years. She always wanted something sweet after a meal, and molasses would satisfy her every time. I watched her many times stir a little butter and molasses together and spread it on that last little bite of bread.

Occasionally we would have to buy lard, but most of the time, we used the homemade lard that was rendered out from the fat skin off the pig Dad had butchered. This was done over an open fire in the big black pot that sat in our backyard. After all the fat was cooked out, the dried pork skins made a very tasty treat.

10

Mom's Typical Day

My mother had to be a very patient and loving woman to raise six children in a two-bedroom house with no plumbing. Getting up at dawn every morning and building a fire in the old wood-burning stove so she could cook breakfast was just a daily routine. A few sticks of wood carefully placed under the stove top and then doused with a bit of coal oil would quickly start a fire and make a hot burner in no time at all. Fresh eggs gathered the day before and a hearty slice of salt-cured ham or sausage patty with freshly made biscuits and gravy was a typical breakfast. Mom would also make a big skillet of fried apples when in season. Leftovers were packed in Dad's lunch pail or a small paper bag for our school lunch. Nothing was wasted.

Having company from out of state was rare, but when we did, Mom always cooked a big dinner. Our table wasn't large enough to seat all the family plus the company, so all the kids had to wait until the grownups were done. We all knew that company came first. Dad had this little way of keeping us from feeling left out while we waited for everyone to finish eating. If we were having chicken, he would give us a fried chicken foot and tell us to go behind the door and eat it. Then he would say, "This will make you beautiful some day!" We never doubted his word! I remember standing behind the door between the dining room and our bedroom many times. Could this be the reason he eventually had five beautiful daughters? Well, I know my other four sisters are beautiful.

Mom wouldn't dream of letting any one of her kids leave the "hollow" wearing dirty clothes. Every one of our dresses were carefully starched and ironed before we left the house to go anywhere. Our baths were taken before bedtime in a large washtub placed in front of the fireplace. The younger children would always bathe first. Hot water was added, until the last child was bathed. Thinking about this, I'm so glad my twin and I were the youngest. We could get pretty dirty playing outside all the time! In the winter, we slept in our underwear; and in the hot summertime, we slept in our home made petticoat or slip.

Keeping up with the sewing for the many dresses the girls needed was a huge chore. As soon as Mom finished with one dress for my twin sister, she had to start all over and make another one just like it for me. This was in addition to the ones she made for the other three girls. She didn't need an exercise machine; the old manual foot-pedal sewing machine kept her legs in great shape. I wonder if Dad ever noticed those beautiful legs.

Dad was a very strict father. If Mom was doing something he thought we should be doing, he scolded us by saying, "Aren't you ashamed of yourself for letting your mother do those dishes? Get in there and help her!" All the chores had to be done before any playing. We carried water from the spring, chopped wood for the cook stove, carried coal in to heat with, fed the chickens and pigs, and washed dishes. And anything else that needed to be done—even sweeping the hard dirt surface of the backyard, which was at times covered with chicken crap.

Without realizing it, Mom taught all her girls many things. Cooking, cleaning, sewing, and saving enough money for a rainy day are three great lessons she taught us that everyone else should know. We were taught to respect our parents and elders. We learned many of life's lessons by just watching Mom and Dad.

11

A Sunny Day Was Washday

Washday was not a fun day. The hot summer months with no rain meant the water barrels were empty and the spring was nearly dry. There was nothing else to do but carry buckets of water up the hill from the pumps at the bottom of the hill. Thank goodness all five girls took turns with this chore! Mom started a fire under the large black kettle in the backyard and instructed us to fill it up. After the water was heated, Mom would dip it out with a bucket and pour it into the washing machine. Then the old, loud gasoline engine (made by Maytag) mounted under the washing tub was started. Occasionally Dad had to help Mom start the engine. The sound of the engine echoed very loudly throughout the hollow as Mom did her laundry. I wonder if she ever thought the noise might wake up the night shift mine workers. But they were probably so tired they never heard a thing. Mom would let us help by feeding the clothes through the ringer into the rinse water and out again. I'll never forget the day our little girl friend was visiting us on laundry day. Her mother had evidently not shown her anything about a washing machine. As she picked up an article of clothing from the washtub and fed it into the wringer, she never let go of the item. Her tiny little arm went through the wringer up to her elbow. We all screamed for Mom. As luck would have it, she ended up with only a few bruises and lots of tears.

Mom always cautioned us not to put our hands near the wash water containing Clorox. One day, however, Mom needed a bottle of Clorox to finish the laundry, so she sent me and my twin sister to the local grocery store. I don't remember how old we were, but everything Mom ever told us was taken literally. On the way home, we accidentally dropped the heavy glass bottle and when it hit the hard pavement it shattered into pieces. (There were no plastic bottles then.) As the liquid splashed all over our legs, we heard Mom's voice saying "Don't get near the Clorox! It will eat you alive!" Believing any minute, we would see holes being eaten into our skin, we began to scream and cry. Then a kind lady living near the road came to our rescue. She quickly wiped off the bleach and assured us nothing was going to happen. Upon arriving home and hearing our dreadful tale, I think Mom finished her laundry without the bleach that day.

Mom always tried to do her laundry on the same day each week, but rainy weather could change her schedule quickly. All the laundry had to be hung on a clothesline to dry outside, and sometimes the weather just wouldn't cooperate. In the winter months when she would take the clothes off the line, they would be frozen so stiff you could stand them in the corner. One thing I could never understand was why Dad stretched the clothesline on the left side of the house when the washer was on the back porch of the right side!

12

Let There Be Light

One of Mom's happiest days was when electricity was connected to our house. She had always dreamed of owning an electric iron, a refrigerator, and an electric stove. My oldest sister helped Mom realize one of her dreams when she bought Mom her first electric iron. The only type of lighting we had before was from coal-oil lamps. On special occasions, Mom would use her Aladdin's lamp. She kept it sitting on top of our big upright piano. This lamp had a glow similar to that of a bright fluorescent light. The tall slender globe and the fragile mantle the lamp contained had to be handled carefully. The mantle inside it would crumble at the slightest touch and was expensive to replace. Mom always thought Dad never cared whether we had electricity or not. And she felt all he worried about was paying the "juice bill," as he called it. My twin sister and I just wanted a refrigerator. We were very jealous of the other school kids when the schoolteachers would let them bring jars of ice cubes to school on the really hot days. Maybe they never knew we didn't have a refrigerator. Mom and Dad were lucky that the electric bill was the only utility bill they ever had to pay.

Our one and only electric stove was given to Mom by her brother when he moved out of Kentucky. At this time, my twin sister and I were the only kids still at home. We were so excited when we were able to cook something without building a fire. Another item Mom's brother left her was an old electric record player with a few large records. My twin and I loved to play the records and sing one of the old songs called "Dance with a Dolly with a Hole in Her Stocking".

13

Homemade Snacks

In the earlier years, a back-to-back fireplace in the living room and in the girl's bedroom heated our home. Later Dad upgraded to a "warm morning heater." He thought this would save money by burning the coal slower. I hated that tall ugly thing standing in the living room hiding our fireplace. I wanted the fireplace back where I could watch the flames as they danced over the red hot coals. On very cold days, we would take turns standing in front of the hot coals and baking our legs until they were red from the heat while turning from front to back.

Sometimes at night before bedtime, one or two of us would get a little hungry. Never having store-bought snacks, we had to find something else to eat; and most of the time, it was a baked potato. Each of us searched for the largest white or sweet potato in the cupboard and placed it in the hot coals of the fireplace to bake. Waiting for them to get done was the hardest part. After about an hour or less, Mom would always help retrieve them from the ashes while warning us how hot the potato could get while baking. I don't recall adding butter, and I can still remember that great taste. They were almost better than candy and a lot healthier!

Hot cocoa on a cold night was also a real treat. This wasn't the kind made from an envelope of instant mix. We used a pot big enough to make a cup for everyone. We measured out the milk, real cocoa, sugar, and a touch of vanilla. Don't let it boil—just get it hot enough to drink.

Another tasty snack we made over the fireplace was parched corn. Kernels of dried corn were roasted over the fire in a heavy cooker until hot and crispy. Eating this was a little hard on the teeth, but it was an excellent way of getting fiber. Every time we had parched corn, Mom probably thought about my sister Gerri. Uncle Monroe, Mom's younger brother, was visiting her when Gerri was just a toddler. He was just a young man and not aware of what was good for babies. Monroe had made himself a snack of parched corn, and as little ones do, Gerri kept reaching for it. Monroe was unaware that she was swallowing the corn whole since she wasn't old enough to have very many teeth. In the middle of the night, she developed a terrific stomachache. Mom found out why the next day when she changed her diaper.

Homemade candy was one of our very special treats. Mom couldn't make it very often because it used so much sugar. But when she did, the box going to our brother in the Navy was the first one filled. Mom loved making fudge and peanut butter roll to mail to her only son. I'm sure his Navy buddies also enjoyed it. The peanut butter roll was my favorite, and I still make it every Christmas. Another easy candy we made was cooking molasses and adding baking soda at the right time. The soda would make the mixture foam very quickly. After cooling it a little, we stretched it into long strips. If we hadn't cooked it just right, we then had a sticky mess.

14

Family Doctor

ittle Doc Combs was known as the camp doctor. He was a small man with a very kind and friendly face. His doctor's office was located upstairs in one of the two-story camp houses near the commissary. Taking care of every family's medical needs from sore throats to delivering babies had to be a responsibility he took very serious. Before I was old enough to know about the birth of babies, I was always told that the stork brought them. The stork in our area was kept very busy, especially by my nearest neighbor. I believe it needed Little Doc's help many times.

No one ever knew when someone was going to need a doctor, and Mom sure wasn't expecting this incident one morning after frying bacon and eggs for our breakfast. Feeding five hungry children was not a simple task! Since our dining room and kitchen were separate areas, Mom couldn't see around the wall from the stove to the table. Trying to hurry, she started to the dining room with a hot skillet of eggs. Mom didn't know my twin sister had left the table and was headed for the kitchen. As they collided with each other, the hot skillet of grease and eggs fell from Mom's hand and spilled all over my sister's face. We were all horrified as we watched our sister stand there and scream from the painful burns. She was crying for cold water to put on the burns, and I couldn't understand why Mom wouldn't give it to her but quickly rushed her to the local doctor. Thinking back, it had to be a miracle that her face healed without any scars since the only medication given for the burns was a small can of cream given to her by Little Doc Combs.

Sometime through the years, I developed a fear of going to a doctor. It may have been from watching Dad having a blood transfusion in the hospital after he was told he had leukemia.

Going to the doctor for me became a big ordeal. I recall climbing up a long flight of steps on the side of the office building with Mom holding my hand. I was scared to death and hated it more than anything. Why was she taking me to the doctor? I only had a sore throat. The doctor greeted us with a kind, friendly voice as he inquired as to why we were there. After filling out some papers, he proceeded to the medicine cabinet remarking, "I can take care of this quickly. Open your mouth," he said. I gagged as he pushed my tongue down with the long flat wooden stick. The smell was sickening, and the deep purple medicine left my tonsils the same color for days. Then it was my twin sister's turn!

Doc Combs was a very likeable doctor, and most any child would rather have him give the required yearly vaccinations instead of the nurse that traveled around the area to each school. There was no kidding around with her. Many times I would make myself sick from worry when the school announced the nurse would be giving shots the next day. The fear that would build up inside me as I stood in the long line waiting for my turn to get a "shot" was more than I could stand. The thought of a needle being stuck deep into my arm was overwhelming. The nurse always tried to make me feel better by saying "This won't hurt." I never believed a word she said! Once while I was walking back upstairs to my classroom, I began feeling sick. I knew I was going to pass out when the sound of bells began ringing in my ears. I laid my head down and later awoke to the strong smell of ammonia under my nose, put there by the teacher. Oh what an embarrassing ordeal! My only thought then was what the cute boy in back of the classroom would think about me now. I never wanted to take another shot!

I've carried that fear of shots for many years. I've been known to pass out in the dentist chair more than once.

15

The Colors of Fall

Autumn—my very favorite time of the year. As a part-time artist, I felt and saw the beauty in the colors of the fall months long before I ever attempted painting on a canvas. The variety of trees covering the surrounding Kentucky Mountains glowed with bright shades of orange, bronze, red, and yellow. I can't help but wonder why Mom never felt the same as I did until she explained to me one day that it was a very sad time when everything to her looked as though it was dying. And maybe it was the thought of preparing for the cold winter months ahead that was always on her mind.

As a child playing outside, I saw beauty in the bright sunlight shining and reflecting through the brightly colored leaves on the different types of trees. My sister and I searched for each color and shape. Finding an open area in the woods to me was like entering a room made with colorful stained glass. But as the sun fell over the mountain range, the colors faded quickly, and my beautiful colors turned gray.

After all the leaves had fallen, I loved being able to see farther into the woods. As the days grew colder, we searched the woods for nuts to add to Mom's homemade fudge. We knew exactly where the hickory nut tree stood. Red berries picked from other trees made pretty Christmas decorations. The small pawpaw bush produced a fruit with the taste of an overly ripe banana. It wasn't one of our favorite treats.

During the summer months there was always some type of flower blooming in the mountains. The spring months brought orange mountain honeysuckle bushes and mountain laurel. Many other small flowers growing close to the ground were violets, wild pansies, and red snake flowers. During the autumn months, the hills were covered with goldenrods and tall bright purple ironweed flowers. Dad could tell without looking at the calendar that it was near the squirrel hunting season when these fall flowers were in bloom. I could see him thinking, "It's time to get the old shotgun cleaned."

All the women looked forward to the new fall Montgomery Ward and Sears catalogues when they arrived at the post office. One would have thought we had a new toy, but this was our "wish book" and our way of window shopping. We couldn't wait to pick out a new pair of shoes for the school season and sometimes a dress or two if Mom had managed to save up a little money. The excitement of the holidays gave the kids something to look forward to. But Dad's mind was only on killing the pig we had fattened up.

November was the time to slaughter the pig and prepare the meat we needed for the winter months. Our main source of meat came from the pigs and chickens we raised. To save on the cost of feeding them, Dad asked the neighbors to save food scraps. These scraps were put in a bucket and left hanging on the post of their back porch outside the kitchen. Animals loved getting into the tasty bucket so everyone hung it so high that we could barely reach it to empty. My sisters and I all hated this embarrassing task of going to each house and collecting the messy scraps. Sometimes as we were pouring the scraps into the pigpen, the pigs would knock the bucket out of our hands as they jumped up on the side of the pen. I was so thankful when Dad did this chore!

The slaughtering always seemed to be on or near Thanksgiving Day. But maybe it was because Dad had this holiday off from the coal mines. I was happy to see this day come. My thinking was no more pigs to feed! Dad never dreamed of sending the hog to a butcher. He would just round up some good old neighbors to help. Then he would make us go inside the house while he shot the hog and cut its throat. The hind feet were tied to a pole and then somehow hung upon a hanger with its head down. The hot water, heated in a large black pot outside, was poured over the carcass. The coarse hair was then easily scraped from the skin with a long newly sharpened butcher knife.

Sometimes we would help with this job, or Dad would just let us think we were helping. When the hair was all scrapped off, the hog looked so fat and naked with its thick white skin. I stood there and watched as Dad cut the belly of the hog down the middle and all the organs fell into a washtub. After several hours, the slaughtering was completed. Every helper and each family that had so faithfully saved the food scraps received a small portion of meat.

To preserve the pork for months ahead, Dad would rub the fresh meat with a thick layer of coarse salt and sometimes sugar. It was then stored on the back porch in an enclosed room. An old saying was "Every part of the pig was used except the squealer." The head was cooked and made into something called head cheese or souse. Even the pig's tail was baked. This I would not eat! But, Mom's homemade sausage was delicious even when it was canned. Dad had turned that pig into ham, bacon, sausage, pork chops, and much more. Meat for the cold winter!

16

The Beauty of Winter

Winter months, though they were harsh at times for parents, brought a special beauty to the mountains. The first snow of the season fell silently, but what an excitement to every child. Sensed by the early morning stillness, one could see before looking out the window the blanket of soft white snow covering everything. On those mornings, my twin sister and I wasted no time piling on the warm clothes while getting ready for school. Quickly we ate our hot breakfast and dashed out the door. We never felt the cold air as we slowly made the first tracks in the snow on our way down the slippery hill. The tree branches over the pathway around the hill hung low from the weight of the heavy wet snow. We felt as though we were walking through a white, frosty fairyland. As we reached up to touch the tiny branches, we laughed as the cold snow softly fell on our faces. Falling up against the hillsides on the soft white blanket, we left behind the prints of snow angels.

Something about the first snow of the season always made everyone happier and friendlier. The boys were throwing snow balls at each other as the girls giggled and covered their heads. I wonder if they saw the beauty that I did. For a moment, everyone forgot we were on our way to school. Quickly we brushed the snow from our coats. We knew we must hurry and leave our fairyland behind to arrive at school before the bell rang. It was very rare for our school to close for a snow day!

When the school day was over, we returned home and continued our playing with the creation of our own sled from Dad's coal shovel. While sitting on the shovel, we held the handle between our legs for steering. We created paths down the hill to imaginary cities where we wanted to go. But all too soon, our trails became a path of ice, making it impossible for anyone to walk up the hill to our house. Dad always took care of that problem very quickly with a bucket of hot cinders from the fireplace, while Mom reminded us patiently to hang up our wet clothes near the fire to dry. Hopefully, a new snow would come again very soon. And then we could make snow ice cream! Mom's rule was to never make ice cream from the first snow. I never understood why!

Painted by Lois Walker West

"Angels in the Snow"

17

Nature's Playground

The surrounding hills became our playground as well as an adventure land for everyone in our little hollow. Very little time for all the neighboring kids was spent inside the house playing since the only toys we had came from Santa once a year.

We became very creative as we searched for the perfect spot for our playhouse. A tree branch with all its leaves was excellent for sweeping an open area clean, and rocks made very good chairs and other pretend furniture for our dolls. We made ourselves skirts and hats from the large cow-cumber leaves that we pinned together with small sticks. Vines hanging from trees made great swings. We couldn't swing as high as Tarzan, but we became quite good at it since we always had a soft bed of leaves to land on should the vine break. Our hike through the hills was a trail of beauty while seeing the wild mountain laurel bushes, the flowering dogwoods, the beautiful orange honeysuckle bushes, and many other numerous plants native to the area. In the late spring, we occasionally ran upon a patch of strawberries. Then we would have to stop and eat awhile.

Even though we knew there were snakes in the hills, we never let that fear stop us from our huge playground. One summer day while we were out picking wild red snake flowers for Mom, we ran upon a very large snake. At first sight, all five girls screamed and began to run down the steep hillside. In our frenzy to get away, my twin sister lost her shoe, and no one was about to turn around and look for it. Later, when we arrived home, Mom wasn't interested in how afraid we were—she just wanted us to find the shoe. She immediately sent us back with orders to *find it!* After walking up and down the hill and having no luck, we returned home and told Mom the snake ate the shoe. For some reason, I don't think she ever believed us.

Our family wasn't the only ones that enjoyed the surrounding hills. Sometimes when we were out playing in the woods, we would come upon a neighbor lady picking wild greens. I don't remember the names of all the greens everyone picked, but we knew of one that we could eat without cooking. It had a really tart but sweet taste and made a nice treat on a beautiful sunny spring day.

When the summers became very hot, our favorite place to play was in front of an abandoned coal mine just down the hill from our house. The cool air from the mine felt as if we were standing in front of an air conditioner. Mom and Dad warned us never to go back into the mine since it was unsafe and overhead rocks were known to fall frequently. They didn't know that it only took one dare from someone to get us inside the mine. But, we didn't make it very far without a flashlight. The unknown darkness ahead sent us running back out very quickly.

It was a lot more fun wading in the cold, clear water running out of the mine creating a soft rippling sound. There we looked for fossils among the rocks and small pieces of black coal. We never realized then the rarity of our finds, only the beauty of the ferns embedded in the small pieces of shiny black coal that had washed out of the old mine.

The area of loose rocks around the walls of the mine was a very good place (according to our oldest sister) to hide and exchange love notes. At that time, I thought this was a very silly thing to do.

My twin sister and I loved playing in the rain on a very warm day. The water running off the housetop was just the right place to wash our hair. Mom never seemed to mind as she handed us a towel to dry with. Maybe we just saved her from filling the old washtub that day. With no gutters on the house, we had many choices as to where we could stand. And of course, we kept our clothes on!

Sometimes after the rain would stop, we would hike up the creek and make a small dam for a swimming hole, but it was a useless task. The fast-moving water down the hill would wash away our small tree branches and rocks as quickly as we placed them.

The heaviest rainstorms could uncover more little treasures. The fast-rushing water down the hills and valleys cleared away most of the dirt from the slate dump across the road from our house and revealed bright yellow clay. Knowing this, as soon as the rain ended we were out searching for the clay. Our clay moldings were not beautiful vases, only small dolls. We left them to bake in the sun on the hot rocks. Some of them were very realistic with the corn silks we used for hair on the body as well as the head. The neighborhood boys never appreciated our talent. They just enjoyed making fun as they threw them at each other. But we rarely caught them in their naughty act.

18

Story Time

An old upright battery radio standing in the living room was our daily outlet to the outside world. When overly tired, Mom would take time out of her busy day to sit down and listen to the daytime soap opera. The nightly news kept everyone updated with the current events. And then, the good shows came on—*The Lone Ranger*, *The Screeching Door*, and our favorite one announcing *Only the Shadow Knows*. We all found ourselves gathered a little closer to the radio and listening very quietly.

Television was not a part of our lives, thus making our imaginations more vivid. On a dark night, lying in bed and listening to the insects outside was always a great time to frighten each other with ghost tales. My twin sister and I were always tucked in between our two older sisters. Having four in the same bed seems a little strange, but none of us were fat! Billie was the most imaginative with her stories. No matter how scary the story became, every tale always ended with the remark "And that's a true story!" It was hard to believe all of them, but I can never forget the ghost story Mom told about seeing her deceased mother standing in the yard of their log cabin while wearing a white dress. Mom was just a young girl at that time and missed her mother very much.

Most every child in the neighborhood loved to read comic books, or "funny books," as we called them. I loved looking at the colorful pictures and found them more interesting to read. Once everyone finished reading them, we would take ten or more books around the neighborhood and trade them for ones we hadn't read. Sometimes we would end up with a new book for an old one, but the condition wasn't the most important thing. We never cared if the pages were a little worn as long as they were readable. Those were the only books I could read all the way through without stopping. I loved Bugs Bunny, Porky Pig, and Archie—no Batman for me! I suppose you could say that the whole neighborhood was our book club.

Dad enjoyed reading the books we brought home from the school library, especially the ones about the old West. But Mom enjoyed the romance magazines the neighbors would give her. I believe that's where she found the name for my oldest sister Doris. Do you think our mom and the neighborhood ladies had their own little book club?

19

Trick or Treat

On Halloween night, kids turning outdoor toilets over and soaping windows were just a few mischievous things that happened.

Then one year just before Halloween, my twin and I heard our friends at school talking about going trick-or-treating. We also heard them tell about getting a bag full of free candy by going from house to house. "Could this really be true?" I don't know why but no one living in our hollow ever went trick-or-treating. After deciding that no one would know who we were if we were all dressed up, we talked each other into trying this game.

Just before dark that night, we searched the house for something to wear. I don't remember asking, and I can't believe Mom let us dress up in the beautiful Japanese kimonos that our brother sent home from Japan when he was in the Navy. One was gray and the other one white. Both had delicate embroidery of bright colorful dragons and other Japanese motifs. We painted our eyes to look slanted with our sister's makeup and smeared red rouge on our faces, hoping to disguise ourselves.

As soon as it was dark, we walked out of the hollow for our first trick or treat night. Now this was Halloween night, and even though we were told trick or treat night was the night before, we thought it wouldn't matter. The first and only house we went to was the home of the post-master in Allais. We were almost too afraid to knock on the door, so we only knocked once. When the door opened, he seemed a little surprised to see us as we mumbled a little trick or treat. He first made us aware of the fact that trick or treat night had already past. Looking at each other, we both knew we were in big trouble. Then he complimented us on our beautiful robes and advised us we probably shouldn't be wearing them out on such an occasion as Halloween. He then invited us in and handed us a treat and told us we should go back home.

After that ordeal, we were too embarrassed to go to another house. We headed back home and decided that was our last and only try at trick-or-treating.

20

Christmas in the Mountains

As the days grew colder, winter was near, and Christmas was only a few weeks away! The first of December to the twenty-fifth had to be the longest time of the year as we anticipated the arrival of Santa. This was the only time of the year we received a real toy. We never asked Santa for much—just a beautiful doll like the ones in the Christmas catalogue or the ones they sold at the ten-cent store in the city of Hazard.

After being reminded a dozen times or more, Dad cut us a beautiful pine tree off the land just across the road. He never told us who owned that property. Maybe it belonged to the coal mining company. Everyone but Dad helped decorate the tree. Mom had bought a few ornaments and silver tinsel, but most of the tree ornaments were hand-made. No electric lights were used in our earlier years, so we were very excited when our brother bought us a string of bubble lights after electricity was installed in the house. My twin and I would sit for hours and watch the sparkling, colorful lights as the liquid bubbled up inside the clear tiny candle-shaped bulbs.

Christmas shopping was never talked about, and the only wrapped packages put under the tree came to us from a relative. But the pages of the Christmas wish book we received in the mail during the early fall were so worn that the book would automatically open to the toy section when anyone picked it up.

One special Christmas, Mom let each of us girls choose the doll we wanted. My twin and I wanted the same beautiful doll wearing a bright red snowsuit. Gerri wanted the one that cried "Momma!" I'm not sure that Billie ever picked out the one she wanted. But I do remember her hating the doll she received that year.

The night before Christmas, we all hung our stockings on large nails we hammered in the mantle over the fireplace. Just any stocking wouldn't do, only the longest one we could possibly find. Sometimes we used Mom's old silk stockings or our long, above-the-knee socks that we wore to school in the winter. We thought the longer the stocking, the more goodies we would get. It was not so, as everyone received the same amount. Each stocking was filled with one apple, one orange, nuts, and candy. I found out many years later that the coal miners' union gave each family enough treats for every child. I don't know how Mom and Dad managed to keep these treats hid until Christmas Eve.

The night before Christmas, Mom had no problem in getting everyone to bed early. One year in the quiet hours of the night, we were awakened as our older sister was filling our stockings. I believe she was a little angry that year and wanted to wake us up purposely. This must have been the first year that Mom and Dad asked her to help. Mom thought she was too old to believe in Santa and receive a doll, but she didn't think so! We were really disappointed it wasn't Santa making all the noise.

Early the next morning, before anyone else was awake, we jumped out of bed, grabbed our stockings off the mantle and our doll from under the tree, and hurried back to bed to eat the treats. Dot was very disappointed that she didn't have a new doll to take to school after Christmas vacation. I believe she hated being the oldest that year and playing Santa.

Mom and Dad tried really hard to make every Christmas a happy one. Baking a cake to leave on top of the old piano for Santa was an essential duty. The next morning, the plate was always empty, and the only thing left was cake crumbs. Through the years, I asked Mom several times, "Who ate all that cake?" She always replied, "Santa".

After the three oldest kids moved away, they would always send Christmas gifts back to the family still at home. My brother and his wife said they always enjoyed picking out dolls for my twin sister and me. I also remember receiving gifts from Mom's brother and his wife in Cincinnati. It was a happy surprise when we would go to the post office and the postmaster would hand us a package. These packages went immediately under the tree and tempted us daily. When Mom wasn't at home, my sister and I would try our best to look through the paper wrapping. Shaking it wasn't good enough either.

One day the mystery finally got to us. We both agreed to never tell anyone as we carefully opened one end of the package and peeked inside. It was a small brown purse. We both felt so guilty.

It was very hard to act surprised on Christmas morning when we already knew what was in that package. Dad never wanted us to open any package before Christmas day! That was the rule then, and today I still keep it!

21

Dad Needs Help

What a terrible day when the doctor told Dad he had a form of leukemia and could no longer work in the mines. Being very young, I did not understand how serious this illness was. Dad had been getting weaker and weaker and found it difficult just to walk home from work. After many tests, the doctors found his blood level was so low that they had to give him transfusions to survive. After years of working in the mines, Dad now realized he could no longer support his family. The remainder of his life was contributed to friends and relatives donating the blood he needed to replace what his body was losing. I remember my brother driving from Cincinnati occasionally just to give him a pint of blood.

Dad never recovered from his illness enough to return to work. I wonder if he felt like a failure while not being able to provide for his family. He was proud and hated accepting charity from anyone, but for a short time, our family received money from the miners' welfare fund. That soon stopped after the welfare department found out Mom had saved a hundred dollars and had opened a small savings account at the bank. I can't imagine her being able to save a dime out of that small amount of money, but I realize now this has been a great inspiration all my life. If she could manage to save money at that difficult time, it made me believe I could do the same.

When the money was stopped, Mom found it necessary to seek employment. Never having worked outside the home, the only type of work she could possibly find was cooking, washing dishes, or ironing clothes. For a short time, she worked at the local laundry ironing shirts and later found employment as a dishwasher in the city of Hazard at May's Grill. Working in the city meant she had to ride a bus to work every day. Mom now became the head of the house. Dad surely must have missed her being at home all the time. He would try to help by walking out of the hollow to meet the bus after work and help her carry the few groceries she had bought at the small market in the city. Mom was a very strong woman, and this was just the beginning of many years working in a restaurant.

22

Anyone Can Make Excuses

Against Mom's wishes, the oldest girl felt it necessary to quit school and seek work to help the family. Or maybe she quit because she just hated school. Shyness was another excuse, and she also felt her clothes weren't as nice as what the other girls were wearing.

The first job she found was working at the local laundry. This only lasted for a short time. She learned very quickly that you do a job the way the boss wants it done! Ironing shirt sleeve after shirt sleeve was not her thing.

"DaTee," as my twin sister and I called her, was like a little mother to all her younger sisters. But the neighborhood boys in our hollow never wanted to cross her path. One morning on her way to school, she ran down the hill; and as she was passing the house of a boy she disliked with a passion, she stepped in a pile of human waste (better known by the four-letter word). Someone living in the camp must have been too lazy to use the outhouse. Suspecting a certain boy and assuming him guilty, DaTee gave the kid a piece of her mind and decided to get even. It didn't take long for her and our first cousin Larry to come up with a scheme. Knowing that all the boys loved playing a game of buried treasurer, she scoped out their hiding place. With the help of our cousin, they shoveled up the first cow patty they came across and put it in the hole where this particular boy hid his treasure. Now all they had to do was sit in the swing on the front porch and watch and wait. It wasn't long before the boys began their buried treasurer game. The satisfaction my sister received that day of watching this kid as he stuck his hand into the hole to retrieve his treasure was one she never forgot. He found his *treasure*, but not exactly the one he expected! A quick look at his hand and the smell told him he needed to head straight for the creek just below the bank on the slate dump. And maybe the cold water cooled him off a bit and cleaned his hand!

My sister Dot was the second child, and then Billie Louise came along. It was impossible for Mom to carry a three-year-old and a baby. So a little jealousy set in when she was told to walk and Billie was now the one being carried all the time. As she grew older, she must have developed a little mean streak. She not only had fights with the boys but also with other girls. She remembers two in particular—one with a girl who was helping her clean up the class room after school and another with a neighborhood girl while walking home from school. I don't know who came out on the winning side. It could have been just all talk.

It was only a few years before Dot stopped fighting the boys and started looking at them in a different way. Now she had eyes for little Willie next door. He looked pretty good to her, but Mom never shared the same feeling. Mom probably disliked every boy who looked at her first daughter. It was a good thing little Willie was old enough to join the Army. Other younger boys in the neighborhood would leave her love notes under special rocks until Dad found out and stopped that immediately. Then there was one named Tommy who lived across the river. He actually wanted her to marry him. She admits now they were too young to even think of marriage.

Dot grew out of her jealousy and felt proud and grown-up now that she was the oldest child at home. David had left home and was now in the Navy. His trips home were very short. He took many pictures of all the family with his new camera and mailed copies back to Mom. Dot was so thrilled when he gave her one of his white Navy hats. She kept and treasured that little hat for many years.

23

A Skinny Shirley Temple

Billie Louise was a tiny little girl with naturally curly hair and the second oldest girl in the family. I can describe her as a skinny Shirley Temple. The other four sisters including myself were all a little jealous because our hair was so straight. If we wanted curly hair, we had to curl it with bobby pins.

I believe Aunt Maggie always felt a little sorry for our sister Billie because she was so tiny. When she lived in Hazard, she would visit our home in the hollow and take Billie home with her on the weekends. Aunt Maggie was a very good seamstress, and Billie always came back with something new. It was almost a necessity that homemakers own a sewing machine. The shops in Hazard sold patterns in any size for any type of clothing along with the fabric.

Since Mom had the pleasure of having five girls, she had to be very thankful for her sister helping her by making clothes for all the girls. I cherish the pictures of me and my twin wearing beautiful navy-blue coats. We were only four or five years old at that time. I would think that making two coats just alike would take a lot of patience.

Billie may have been small, but she was very smart in school. The schools recognized her exceptional abilities during her grade school years and let her skip a year, which put her in the same grade with Dot. Aunt Maggie may have contributed to her extra learning skills during the times she spent at her house. She learned to read quickly and loved the books our Aunt bought her.

Even though Billie was smart, she did have her other little faults. She made Gerri so mad one day that she picked up a jar of marbles and threw it at Billie. It just missed Billie's head, and marbles went flying everywhere. She now swears that Gerri was trying to kill her. That must have been an incident displaying the Walker *temper* Mom talked about.

There were times when Billie's stubbornness was worse than a mule. It never seemed to matter how hard Mom would spank her, she would never cry. Many times she would remark, "Just beat me to death. I don't care." I'm sure Mom never whipped her very hard since she was so little, and that tiny little branch off the tree only stung our legs for a short time.

One of the most eventful stories Billie ever told happened at the first house Mom and Dad owned. This small little house was located as far up the hollow as one could go. One day Mom sent Dot down to the spring where she kept the milk. Overhearing Mom, Billie ran ahead of her big sister toward the spring. The cold water here ran out of the mountain into a large barrel. Mom had lowered a container of fresh milk down into the barrel to keep it cold. This was Dad's substitute for a refrigerator! Billie reached the barrel just ahead of Dot. As she leaned over tugging on the rope that held the heavy milk, she fell headfirst into the barrel and couldn't get out. The only thing our sister Dot could see were her legs sticking out. Dot arrived just in time to grab her feet and pull her out. Even to this day, Billie always gives Dot the credit for saving her life.

Another story she loved to tell was about her and Dot climbing the cherry tree. This also happened at the same little house. The tree was one of their favorite places to play especially when the cherries were starting to get ripe. Since both of them loved to go barefoot, Billie grabbed a bed pillow one day and ran outside to play. Climbing the tree carefully, they placed the pillow on a branch where both could stand and jump up and down and enjoy the juicy red fruit. Just as Dot was pulling down a limb to pluck the biggest red cherry on the tree, they heard the sound of the limb cracking as it split and fell to the ground with both of them hanging on. Terrified of what Dad might do, they tried to think up a story to explain what had happened. But to their surprise, he never said a word. Maybe he didn't like cherries! Mom heard the noise and ran outside. She grabbed the pillow and explained she wanted to wash it since it was used when Uncle Burtis died and they put his head on it when his body was placed on a door on the sofa.

Hearing this, it upset Billie more than breaking the limb off the cherry tree. After that she said she had nightmares!

Many years later because of Dad's sickness, Aunt Maggie wanted to help the family out by taking Billie to live with her in Franklin, Ohio, at the age of fifteen. She attended school there and graduated from Monroe High School in 1952. Dot also lived with Aunt Maggie and was working at a supermarket when she met a young man and later married him.

24

The Middle Girl

Gerri wasn't actually the middle child, but she was the middle girl. She was definitely more independent than the other four girls. Could we most likely have forced this upon her by some of our unfair treatment? Being the middle girl couldn't have been easy. Dot and Billie, the two older girls, were always chumming together. On the other side, she had me and my twin sister to deal with. We all loved her, but we made her life a little miserable at times. Early one morning, Gerri hurried out of bed to go to the outhouse. While she was gone, Joyce and I locked the door and wouldn't let her back inside. She knocked and pounded on the door, yelling, "Let me in!" It wasn't long before Dad was awakened by all the noise. We knew immediately that we were in big trouble. We ran upstairs and tried to hide, but it wasn't long before Dad found us. Dad never wanted to whip the girls, but this was one time he had no problem. He usually left this job up to Mom. Today we try to make allowances to Gerri for all the bad things we did to her. After all, now she's not afraid to go anywhere alone and will tackle anything. She's an independent woman who made it very well on her own.

If either of our sisters made Joyce and me mad, they had both of us to contend with. I can still hear Gerri yelling, "Mom, they're both on me!" Gerri learned at a very early age that all it took to get her way was to turn on the tears. She chose her friends among kids that lived outside the hollow. She always wanted the better things in life. She never left the house without her hair being curled. Every night before going to bed, she rolled her hair up in little curls and pinned them with bobby pins. By the time she was finished, she had used every bobby pin in the house. If anyone else wanted to curl their hair, they had to use strips of rags or metal strips cut from a tin can that was wrapped with cloth. The rag strips were especially good to make beautiful curls with long hair. It was told that one of our neighbors once used a hot poker to curl her daughter's hair. I'm sure this was a lot cheaper than going to the beauty shop and letting the beautician hook you up to electric rollers. This was the latest way of getting a permanent wave. I wanted no part of anything hot being used on my head! Those women looked as though they were sitting in an electric chair, but Dot was brave enough to try it when she was about eight years old.

Gerri was very popular in high school and wanted to attend every school dance. Knowing Mom couldn't afford to buy the formal dresses she needed for a dance, her friends were always ready to loan her a gown. I thought she looked like a fairy princess all dressed up walking out of the hollow to meet her date. Gerri had to be someone special; after all, she dated the same boy all through high school.

It was a rare occasion when our boyfriends came to the house to pick us up. If they made it up the hollow and past all the barking dogs, we were lucky if they ever wanted to take us out again. We wouldn't think of asking them to walk us home after dark. But if they insisted, we prayed they wouldn't get lost on the small path around the hill. Just one step too close to the edge of the path and they were likely to fall over the hill. We had traveled it so many times that even on a moonless night the path was familiar.

Gerri had many friends at the little church we all attended. She loved singing in the choir and attending special functions the young people would have. They were always having parties.

25

Who's Who?

It was really hard to believe when my dad told everyone he could not tell his own twins apart. Everyone needs a twin, if it could make their childhood as happy as ours was. I will never know the feeling of not having someone who is exactly like yourself around you all the time. Someone who thinks like you, dresses like you, and loves the same things as you do. Growing up in Kentucky, we were two very skinny little girls who looked exactly alike. No one could tell us apart, and no one ever called us by our real names. It was always "Little Twin."

Every day after school, you could see us walking up the hollow and holding each other's hand as though we might get lost from one another. Maybe that's what Mom told us to do when we were little. As we grew older, we found ourselves getting embarrassed when we heard people making remarks about us holding hands. Mom always insisted on dressing us exactly alike, which made it more likely that people would notice us.

Our feelings for each other were so close that there are times, even today, that we cannot agree on certain incidents. One particular incident was about buttermilk! I remember crying for some buttermilk knowing very well that Mom did not have any. In a fit of anger, I fell backward and cut the back of my head. Today, Joyce will tell you the same story, and it's all about her. Even though many years have gone by, we still can't agree which one of us received this injury. But I believe I have the scar!

I don't believe we ever felt each other's pain. But one time when Mom was pulling Joyce's tooth, I climbed behind the couch and fainted. I don't know why; it wasn't hurting me. I was wandering if I was going to be next. One of the strangest things we did when we were very young was call each other by the same nickname of "Gau'kee." I don't know what we were trying to say, but it sounded the same no matter who was talking. Today our voices still sound alike, and many people still say they can't tell us apart.

Everyone in our family will agree that they spoiled us rotten! If we didn't always get our way, we would fall in the floor and kick our heels screaming. Mom would just walk away leaving the older children to console and pet us like they always did. On a rare occasion, we were known to fall asleep on the floor behind the door. But this was only after we called out for someone to console us and no one came.

I don't remember ever spending a night away from each other, even during our teenage years. If one of us did get invited to spend a night with a girlfriend, we both went. We were stared at so much in public that we felt like monkeys in a cage. And it still amazes us how many people ask "Are you twins?"

26

Good-bye, Kentucky; Hello, World

Most of the stories I know about my brother I was told by members of my family. My brother, David, was the oldest child. After the fifth sister arrived, he was probably thinking, *Not another girl!* Five sisters I'm sure were more than enough. Maybe that's the reason he left home at fourteen. My twin and I called him "Bubby." Dot, the oldest girl, still feels terrible because she caused him to get a terrible whipping from Dad. One summer David had planted his own little watermelon patch. He was very proud as he watched the melons grow and waited patiently for them to grow big enough to eat. He didn't know it then, but Dot was also watching them! One day when David was gone, Dot took a sharp knife to the patch and cut a small hole in each melon, trying to find one ripe enough to eat. After all, this is what the grocery store did when we bought one there. When David found out what Dot had done, there was no reasoning with him; he was ready to kill her. He tried to explain it all to Dad, but nothing he said helped the situation. Dad had to calm him down with a good whipping.

Even as a small boy, David loved his toy airplanes. When he was big enough to put a model kit together, he would spend hours in his attic room gluing together the small precut pieces of wood. The final finishing step of the tiny model was to cover it completely with thin tissue paper. He was so proud of his work, but he found out the hard way that these models were not meant to fly. Opening the small window in the attic, he carefully sailed the little plane toward the sky. Running outside, he found his hard work crushed beyond repair on the ground. But this never stopped him from building another one.

David never gave up the idea of flying. He actually thought he could fly at one time. Mom caught him one day on top of the house with a blanket tied around his shoulders ready to jump. After persuading him to come down, she explained to him that Superman in the comic books was not real. Mom saved him that day, but she wasn't quite ready for the next one.

With the help of some other boys, he rigged a cable to a large tree and then down the hill to another. Placing a stick across the cable and holding on to each side, he glided down the hill a little faster than he expected. It was very ingenious, but he was only a small boy having fun without realizing the stick was wearing thin from the friction. His fun ended quickly when the stick broke and so did his arm.

David was only fourteen years old when he left home. He had grown to love his sisters as much as we loved him, but he felt he must get away from the coal mining area. He found his opportunity when Grandpa Wooton invited him to go to Cincinnati with him on the train to visit Aunt Tenny. Since this was during World War II, many jobs were available, and his age wasn't an issue. David decided to stay in Cincinnati and found work in a shoe factory. He had also found his way out of the coal mining community, and his fear of working underground was gone.

27

A Moving Outhouse

One of my most memorable trips was riding a steam engine train from Hazard to Cincinnati to visit our brother David. Joyce and I were only five years old at that time, and this was our first trip outside the state of Kentucky. We had to ride the city bus from Allais to the train station in Hazard with our bags. After Mom bought our tickets, we stood outside along the train, waiting until we heard the man call out "All aboard!" Mom quickly helped us up the steps to enter the train. We had seen lots of trains in Allais hauling coal, but this one was different. We were amazed that people could ride on a train and also walk up and down the aisles while the train was moving. We really had no idea where we were going or how long it would take to get to Ohio. On board, Joyce and I wanted to play up and down the aisles, but Mom wouldn't let us out of her sight.

Soon, like any other child, we had to use the outhouse. We thought the train would stop and let us off, but that didn't happen. The man who took our tickets showed Mom the direction toward the bathroom. Were we ever surprised when Mom walked us to the bathroom on board! I can still remember looking down in the toilet and seeing the ground whizzing by underneath us. It was a moving outhouse! Since we were too afraid to sit down over the hole, Mom had to hold us up. I'm sure glad I didn't fall through that hole.

Many hours passed before we arrived in Cincinnati. As the train slowed down and entered the huge station, Joyce and I felt a little afraid and excited at the same time. Mom was looking all around, trying to find David. Then she heard his voice. He came running toward her as she pushed her way through the crowd toward him. After giving all of us a big hug, David led the way out of the station. Our long train trip was over, but our adventure in Cincinnati was only beginning.

One day David took us downtown Cincinnati on a streetcar to the huge department stores in the city. David was just a young boy and had lots of energy. Walking everywhere through the city, Joyce and I became very tired. Riding the elevators up and down in the large stores had made us dizzy and sick to our stomach. But Mom thought we were sick from the vaccination the doctor gave us, which was required before we could start school that year. David tried to help by taking turns carrying us one at a time. Needless to say, our shopping trip was cut short that day.

Back at Aunt Tenny's house, we were scared to death by her huge German shepherd dog. One day when Joyce and I were being a little too noisy, the dog started growling at us. We had never been around a dog so big! The dog started barking loudly, and we ran to the living room and jumped behind the couch. The dog followed and also jumped on the couch and looked down at us. The chase continued through her small apartment from room to room as we screamed for help. The dog chased us, and Mom chased the dog. We thought the dog hated us, but our aunt said it only wanted to play. After our visit with Aunt Tenny and David, I'm not sure how we made it back to Allais.

28

First Day of School

Everybody remembers their first day of school, and mine is no exception. It started out being very exciting as my twin and I walked out of the hollow with our older sisters. Then it ended being a very traumatic and memorable day. The lower grade school had two first-grade classrooms—there were no kindergarten classes in those days. It was rumored that one of the first-grade teachers was noted for failing kids simply because she liked them and wanted them to stay in her class another year. So Mom gave strict instructions to my older sister to make sure my twin and I were not put in that classroom. Naturally, this is where we were assigned. When the first recess came around and our sister found out what had happened, she immediately marched us to the other classroom and told the teacher what our mother had said. The teacher then told the principal. It wasn't long before he came into the room and proceeded to try and take my twin and me back to the other room. Now, being the sweet angels we were, we had made up our minds that we were not going back. We both fell to the floor in the hall, lying flat on our backs while we kicked our heels on the floor, crying to the top of our voices. There probably wasn't a classroom in the school that couldn't hear us. But this was stopped very quickly when the principal jerked us up off the floor, spanked our behinds, and placed us once more in "that other room." Could that temper tantrum have kept us from being her favorite students and possibly made her glad to pass us on to the next grade at the end of that year?

The lower grade schools as well as the high school we attended in Kentucky had very good teachers. The children respected them and knew if they didn't behave they would be spanked or sent to the principal's office. The desk where we sat and the books we used were assigned at the beginning of each school season. We were not allowed to write in the books or on the desk. We could not chew gum in class or talk unless spoken to. Homework was assigned almost every day. Final exams were given at the end of each year. If one had made excellent grades through the year, you would be exempt from taking the exams. Students were well-prepared after graduating from high school to go out and find a job. The ones who could afford it continued their education. Many students excelled at their jobs later in life as teachers, lawyers, doctors, and government workers.

29

Friendly Neighbors

I can still hear my neighbor next door when she would call out loudly from her back porch, "Little Twin! Can you babysit?"

Babysitting with the neighbor's kids wasn't for money. My twin and I loved to play with the baby and all her other small children. We weren't very old ourselves and knew it was impossible for Polly to take all five of her small children with her grocery shopping. This was probably the only way she ever managed to find time away from her house. On her way out the door, she always said, "I won't be gone long." On some days this would turn into several hours. But we considered the pay excellent when she returned and gave us twenty-five cents or a candy bar.

I believe she had a new baby every year. The last time I counted, she had seven children. I thought she was normally fat until one day she had a new baby and suddenly became thin again. That was the day I suspected the stork did not bring babies. The word *pregnant* was never used around children. Even when our dogs were ready to have puppies, Mom and Dad would lock them up in the chicken house, and we were not allowed to go near them.

Now I understand why my older sisters at one time thought you could get pregnant by kissing a boy. But this wasn't the case for very long. They soon learned by attending parties what kissing was all about. Teenage birthday parties were the favorite functions to attend. And playing the game of "spin the bottle" or "post office" was where most every young boy or girl received their first kiss. It may not have been with the boy or girl you wished for, but it was the feeling of being a grown-up. Sitting in a circle and waiting for the spinning bottle to stop and point was sometimes a mixture of excitement or horror, depending on the spinner! If it was a cute boy, you might spend a long time in the post office. Then the appointed postmaster would take charge and check to see if there was a problem inside! Usually, two little red shy faces left the room quickly and returned to their seats. And the mother may enter the room and suggest everyone play a new game.

30

School's Out!

What child doesn't look forward to the end of the school year and summertime? We knew summer had officially arrived when we were allowed to take our shoes off and feel the warm earth beneath our feet. Most every kid in the neighborhood went barefoot in the summer. Parents never seemed to mind until it was bedtime and then all we heard was "Look at those dirty feet." What the heck! It saved parents a little money on shoes.

Summertime entertainment might be going to a traveling carnival. Our big problem was finding someone we knew with a car to drive us there. That didn't happen too often. Oh, the thrill of seeing the brightly colored lights was breathtaking, and the ride on the merry-go-round was one we talked about endlessly! We loved the cotton candy and the little plastic dolls with the feathers stuck on their head, but the merry-go-round was the best of all. Riding the ponies as they moved up and down to the sound of the loud music and the bright lights overhead put us in a magical world of our own, but it only lasted for a very short time.

It wasn't very often that we had company, but when we did it was only in the summer months. We never connected the fact that people working for big companies gave you time off for vacations. Occasionally our aunt Maggie would come for a visit from Ohio. We thought she was rich, having a car and all. If we were lucky, she would pile all of us in her car and drive us to Big Creek to see Aunt Emma. She was a sister to Mom and Maggie. The trip over the mountains took hours, and the curves in the road became worse the farther we went. Soon our stomachs began to churn from the swaying of the car around each corner. The motion sickness was more than we could stand. The narrow roads through the mountains left very little room for a car to pull off along the roadside. There was nothing left to do except roll the window down and stick your head out and hope the upchuck missed the side of the car. Sometimes it ended up in the car, and then we all became sick!

Once we arrived, it didn't take long to recover from the sickness. Aunt Emma always had a big dinner cooked, and none of us had any problem in eating. One of the farms where she lived was located near a river. While swimming one day, Billie had the scare of her life when a lizard-like creature crawled up her bathing suit. Then she was embarrassed to death after realizing Jimmy and Wayne, our cousins, were watching when she quickly pulled her bathing suit off to get rid of the creature. Those boys then had the laugh of their life. I don't know what she was worried about. Being so skinny, she couldn't have had much to look at!

Since Joyce and I did not know how to swim, the deep river was off limit for us. We just loved wading in the warm, shallow, rippling stream at the edge of the river, except for the one time we looked down and saw red slimy leaches clinging to our legs. We started crying and screaming so loud that everyone thought a snake had a hold of us. We couldn't get out of that water fast enough. Our cousin Magdalene kept assuring us the leaches were harmless as she quickly pulled each one off our legs. She told us never to go into that part of the river again.

Other than a few unfortunate incidents, we had many hours of fun floating on old tubes and playing in the river. A little farther down the river hung a swinging bridge. We were very careful not to cross the bridge if someone else was on it, as it was a little terrifying if the bridge began swinging back and forth. Sometimes the older boys and girls would purposely jump up and down to scare anyone crossing the bridge.

One day after running across the bridge, I fell on a pile of old barbed wire and stuck the sharp barbs in my leg. As I lay there screaming, Joyce ran for help. When she returned, she wanted to help me so bad. Then without even thinking, she quickly pulled the wire from my leg before I could say a word. The blood started pouring from my leg. I believe it was Dot that carried me to Aunt Emma's house. A little bandage took care of the wound, and I was once again out playing.

The summers weren't all fun and games in the country. Aunt Emma, Aunt Lillie, and Aunt Dorothy all lived fairly close to one another. They all raised acres of corn and tobacco, and our visits always seemed to be just at the time the crops needed hoeing. Once again, my twin and I got out of another job the older girls were told to do. Picking the large ugly green horned worms off the tobacco plants and smashing them with rocks was the very most terrible thing to do.

Joyce and I just enjoyed the June apple tree near the garden. This was one of the first apples in the summer to get ripe. Occasionally we had to watch out for a big bull. The apple tree was in his territory inside the fence. If he started chasing us, we had to climb through the fence quickly! He must have liked those apples too!

To get away from the small kids, the older girls would take long walks with our cousin Mary, Tenny or Magdalene down the dusty dirt road to the post office. The younger kids were never invited on these trips. We later realized their trips weren't just to get the mail; they were hoping to see some cute boys on the way. Sometimes they were lucky, which made their trip worth the walk. Puppy love was sometimes sparked but ended quickly at the end of summer. It was on one of these walks that Mary told Dot and Billie about the birds and the bees. Our parents never discussed the facts of life with their children. I believe all the kids just passed the word around. Usually it was an older playmate telling a younger one.

31

You Want Me to Wring a Chicken's Neck?

Since Mom was forced to work outside the home, all five girls learned to cook at an early age. It was either learn to cook or starve since fast-food places were unheard of. The money Mom earned working was used only for the main necessities-such as clothing, cleaning products, and the food items we could not grow in the garden.

One day while Mom was away, someone suggested cooking fried chicken. Now to fix chicken wasn't quite as easy as it is today. Since we didn't have any money to go to the market, we decided to go outside and catch one of our very own farm-raised chickens. Maybe it was the untimely feeding that made the chickens suspicious as we tried to creep close enough to grab one. But I believe those chickens knew exactly what we wanted for dinner, and they were not about to cooperate. Time after time, just as we were close enough to grab one, off they would run, all in different directions!

Then we all decided there was nothing left to do except chase one down. All eyes were focused on one particular chicken as we chased it all over the yard. I don't know who was panting the hardest when the chase was over—the chicken or us. By the time we finally caught one, we had a very hardy appetite.

Now the big question: Which one is going to kill the chicken? Mom had always made it look so easy. She simply grabbed the chicken by the neck, swung it around, and with a quick snap of the wrist, the neck was quickly broken. Dot, being the oldest and strongest, said, "I can do it!" Now she had the part of swinging it around just right, but when it came to the snapping of the neck, she just wasn't strong enough. Then Billie tried her hand at it and also came up a failure. I imagine the poor chicken was pretty dizzy by this time. From this point on, I'm not sure which story is true. Some of us remember the chicken running away, and others remember someone chopping the chicken's head off with a hatchet and throwing it under a washtub! I don't believe anyone of us would have had enough nerve to swing that hatchet! If we did and managed to get it cleaned, cut up, and fried, I wonder if anyone of us could even recognize what part of the chicken we were eating. Note: Dot now remembers choking the chicken to death, throwing it under the tub to keep it from flopping away, cleaning it, frying it, and we all ate it!

Our chickens may not have been truly organic, but the taste of a free-range frying chicken is one you can't find in a supermarket today. The ones our family raised were from the eggs we gathered daily out of the nests. Mom realized quickly, when an old hen wouldn't get off the nest, that she was ready to sit on the eggs and hatch out baby chicks, or doodles, as we called them. Mom would select just the right number of eggs to add to the nest. It was up to the hen to make sure every egg was kept covered and warm. The mother hen would stay on the nest day and night and only leave it long enough to eat. This process only took twenty-one days. After all the eggs hatched and the doodles were old enough, they would leave the nest with the momma hen. Joyce and I loved following them around the yard. We waited for a chance to pick one up, but that didn't happen very often. Mom was afraid we might squeeze them too hard and make them die. When we did catch one, we only held it a very short moment.

During the spring months some families ordered their baby chicks from catalogues. The post office at times was filled with boxes of doodles - each box had it's own food and water supply. Having to put up with all the noise they were making, I'm sure the postmaster wasn't very happy when this happened.

32

Front Porch Stage

At the age of sixteen and still in Cincinnati, David informed Mom and Dad that he wanted to sign up and join the Navy. He knew he needed their approval since he was underage. Mom was so glad the war had just ended; this most likely helped Mom and Dad as they signed that approval form. I often wonder why he chose the Navy instead of the Air Force, knowing his love for airplanes. He stayed in the Navy for four years before returning to Cincinnati to marry his first love.

I was only eight or nine years old when David brought Elaine, her sister, and her Mom and Dad to Allais to meet all of his family. The thoughts that must have run through her mind as she neared this coal mining community had to be terrible. She was a city girl who grew up on the streets of Cincinnati where sidewalks existed! We had never seen anyone so beautiful. Her long black hair was curled softly over her shoulders, and her clothes looked as though she had just stepped off the pages of the Sears or Montgomery Ward catalogue.

Elaine's mom and dad were terrific people. If they had any negative thoughts of the area, no one ever knew. The men were busy carrying electric guitars and large speakers up the steep hill to our front porch. David evidently had neglected telling anyone that our house wasn't wired with electricity. It only took a few minutes to realize something was wrong. But David and Dad wasn't about to let that stop the music! Dad rigged up a place to plug in the speakers from the neighbor's electrical outlet by using several extension cords. The front porch across the front of our house was turned into a stage. It sat higher on the hill than the other houses, making it the perfect place for everyone in the mining camp to hear the music. The sounds filled the hollow with echoes that no one had ever heard before. Elaine and her dad played and sang music until late in the night. Joyce and I joined in, singing our favorite song titled "I Wish I Was Single Again." The entertainment that night was better than the Grand Ole Opry from Nashville.

Elaine's sister Ruth was younger, but just as beautiful. She didn't seem to be as musically talented as Elaine, but I'll never forget the beautiful paper dolls she drew for us. She could have been a fashion designer. Sometimes Mom would buy us paper dolls from the ten-cent store, but most of the time, we cut them from last year's catalogue. We could actually find clothes to fit these dolls if we looked through the catalogue long enough. The models had to be standing in the same position in order for the paper clothes to fit. After we were through cutting up the catalogue, it was ready for the outhouse.

Our lives were never quite the same after our company left. I think we all felt there was a more exciting place to live than in our own little hollow, and we knew David had already discovered that. Pretty clothes became a reality for Billie when Elaine accidentally left behind her blue satin slip. Billie cherished that soft, silky slip until the day she accidently left a brown scorched imprint on it from a hot iron. After crying a few tears, she decided to wear it anyway!

33

More Visitors from Ohio

After leaving Kentucky, my two older sisters moved in with Aunt Maggie. My sister Dot was a very pretty young girl. While working and living in Ohio, it wasn't very long before she met a handsome young man and was married. Being very proud of her new husband, Dot brought Bob and his mother to Kentucky for a visit. They had never, to my knowledge, stayed with anyone who didn't have a bathroom in the house. Mom gave up her bed to the newlyweds, and Mrs. Cook had to sleep in the room with all the other girls. Now this was a very small room with two double beds. Mom and my sister Geraldine slept in one bed, and Mrs. Cook wanted to sleep with the twins. Billie was living with Aunt Maggie at this time. We thought it was funny when she asks us if we were going to sleep in our panties. She also wanted to know where our pajamas were. It took her a while to understand that our undershirts and panties *were* our pajamas.

She was also very concerned about what to do if she had to use the bathroom in the middle of the night. We told her to just go outside in the yard like we did. This did not appeal to her at all. We could see the fear in her face at the thought of a wildcat coming down out of the mountains, especially since we had shared the story of a wildcat killing our small dog on the porch. We offered her a flashlight, but that wasn't the answer either. After thinking through the alternatives, she was not about to go outside after dark! Mom finally resorted to bringing out the old "slop jar" or bedside potty from the attic and put it beside her bed. I don't know if she used it or not. She may have not slept very much, but she made it through the night. That next morning, she got up and surprised us all by making homemade doughnuts. But Mom fixed her usual breakfast of biscuits, gravy, sausage and eggs, or sometimes fried chicken. Boy was Mrs. Cook shocked at that! I don't know why she never wanted to visit us again.

34

Dad's Love for Kentucky

My father evidently had no desire to live anywhere except Kentucky. Mom said she felt as though he wanted to keep her as far up in the hollow as possible and away from everyone. Maybe he just wanted her all to himself and didn't want her to look at another man. Dad was a coal miner when he and Mom were married, and he was also a very good handyman around the house. When Dad inherited land from his father, he built the foundation of their first home from limestone rocks he and his brother chiseled out of the mountain. Maybe it was one of these times that Dad saw his brother die from a heart attack upon the mountain.

Most of my memories living in the Allais area are from the years my family lived in their second home. It had a clear view of the road leading in and out of the hollow. I can still see the miners walking home in their work clothes covered with the black coal dust from the mines and the carbide lights attached to their hard hats. The carbide lights were used by every miner and were the only means of seeing in the dark mines. This had to be a dreadful job working underground. I don't imagine they saw too many daylight hours when working the day shift. My twin sister and I always looked forward to the hour when Dad would arrive home. He would give us a big hug and hand over his metal lunch box containing the treat he had saved for us. What a simple little way of showing us his love!

Hearing Dad's laughter is one of my great memories. But the family never knew what kind of mood he was going to be in when he was drinking. I know he must have loved music. Mom said on many occasions he would pay someone to play our old piano or an old guitar for him. Sometimes when he had a little too much to drink, it would make him happy and he would do a hoedown, stomp tap dance. He had great rhythm! He always gave everyone the impression that he was very proud of all his children. When he would bring a friend home, he would have Dot play our old upright piano. Then we would gather around and sing the songs he loved to hear.

Other times when he would come home drunk, he would sit on the porch and ramble on for hours talking about someone or something he was mad about. Billie was usually the one who would sit and listen to him. He never seemed to have enough courage to give any of us advice concerning boys unless he was drunk. And even then he could only say "If you ever get yourself in trouble, I would just as soon see you dead and you know what I mean!" That was enough to put the fear in all of us!

The worst fear my sisters and I have of Dad's drinking was when he accidentally shot a hole in his bedroom ceiling. This was an occasion when someone had made him mad before he came home that night. The shot woke us up, and Mom hurried all of us to the neighbors that night. The next day, Dad acted as though nothing had happened. Surely he must have remembered something! But I don't remember anyone even talking about it later.

Dad loved to play poker and gamble with his friends. It was told that he lost one of his shotguns in a poker game. He must have been a serious poker player. Because of his gambling, he would never allow his girls to play with gambling cards. But our neighbor, Polly, loved for Dot and Billie to visit her and play Rook. Sometimes these games went on for hours, and Mom would send someone to Polly's house to tell them to come home. But most of the time, we would just walk outside and call loudly from the porch!

One of the things Dad loved to do most was squirrel hunting at Red River, Kentucky. Most of the time, he had some of his local friends to go hunting with; but on occasion, he would take a younger boy (or man) and teach him a few of his hunting tricks. Our cousin Wayne was one of these kids.

Modern day campers equipped with kitchen facilities and bathrooms did not exist in those early years. Their campsites were usually at the base of a cliff under the shelter of a huge rock or cave. Once an excellent spot was found, I'm sure they returned there time after time. I don't know who had the camera, but many years later, I found pictures of their camp site. I can imagine the tall tales everyone told while sitting around the campfire. I wonder if Dad ever felt bad about going away and leaving his family; he was in a sense providing food for them. The fuzzy red squirrel tails were Dad's special prizes for his kids. We learned to love the squirrels Mom cooked in gravy after his many hunting trips. Dad would skin the squirrels and remove all the hair, and Mom would do the cooking. The cooking of the squirrels included even the heads. I've seen the time when someone would get upset if there weren't enough squirrel heads to go around. After all, taking a spoon and cracking open the skull to taste the delicate brains was, at that time, uh, delicious.

35

Mom's Scary Night

Growing up in the mining camp at Allais, Kentucky offered very little night-time entertainment. Mom wasn't very good at making up bedtime stories, but sometimes she loved telling us stories about her early years of taking care of six children.

This event happened one night while Dad was away. Mom told us she had the scare of her life. It took place when she lived in her first home up the hollow. The night began like most any other night. After putting all her children to bed, she sat down to relax and read a magazine. The stillness of the night was soon shattered by the noise of something on the tin roof. Mom sat motionless with thoughts of terrible things running through her mind as she listened to the *tap, tap, tap* and then the long scratching sounds. Dad was due back anytime, but that didn't ease the fears Mom was having at the moment. The fear of not knowing what was outside was more than she could take. She knew she had to protect her children and find out what was out there. Looking around the room, the only thing she could find for a weapon was the broom standing in the corner. Holding the broom tightly, she quietly opened the living room door and stepped softly across the porch and out into the yard where she could look and see the top of the house. What a sigh of relief when she looked up and the only thing she saw was a young turkey that Dad had bought a few weeks earlier. It was climbing up the tin roof, losing its footing and sliding down time and time again. Dad probably laughed at her when she told him that scary tale!

I always loved hearing Mom's stories during her visits to me in Ohio. When I asked her questions, it encouraged her to tell me new events.

36

Sunday Was Church Day

Sunday was a day when everyone put on their best clothes and went to church. I love seeing old pictures of my Dad in his Stetson hat and dress clothes. He never went anywhere without that hat, and there were no blue jeans for him. It was unthinkable for retail stores to stay open on the day of rest. Most families cooked a big Sunday dinner, and all the family was there to sit around the table and eat after attending church. I don't think Mom or any other mother had much rest after all that cooking. Attending church was an important part of our lives as we grew up in Kentucky. The church we attended was named the Petrey Memorial Baptist Church. I don't remember Dad ever going to church, but Mom told us he was a faithful attendee in the early years of their marriage. He joined the church and enjoyed singing in the choir. While working in the coal mine, I believe he always felt that God watched over him. He told us a story once about hearing a voice telling him to step back, and just a moment later, a huge rock fell right where he had been standing. Dad worked in the coal mine until he became sick with leukemia. My brother David moved Mom and Dad to Middletown, Ohio, in 1956. The leukemia was in remission when suddenly Dad was killed in a car accident in 1959 while on a fishing trip. Mom remained in Middletown for many years and never remarried. My sisters and brother all lived in the Middletown and Cincinnati area after leaving Kentucky. Mom was blessed with fifteen grandchildren. Dad never enjoyed living in Ohio, but he lived long enough to see my brother's son born in Cincinnati. That day I could see that Dad was the proudest person alive. He now had a grandson to carry on the Walker name.

From the information I've been given through the years, the Walkers originally came from Edinburgh, Scotland, in the early 1600s. They were among the first pioneers to settle in Eastern Kentucky. Someone once said that when you make an acquaintance with a Walker, you have made a friend for life. I want to think that this is true!

Today all of Mom and Dad's descendants live outside the state of Kentucky. Many years later, the big white house burned to the ground, and the land was sold. The hollow as I knew it doesn't exist anymore. But I hope my story will keep the memories alive for years to come.

About the Author

Lois grew up in Allais, Kentucky, a small coal-mining community near Hazard. She moved to Ohio in 1956 following her graduation from Hazard High. She remained in Ohio, working and raising her family; and after the retirement and death of her husband, she moved to Monticello, Florida, in 2003 to help in the care of her mother who passed away in 2005. Her desire to pass on her love for Kentucky and her many happy childhood memories surfaced and inspired her writings when her children and later grandchildren began questioning her about the olden days of growing up in the hills of Kentucky. Since her parents only talked briefly of their early years, Lois wanted to pass hers down in written form. She has an identical twin sister named Joyce, who shares many of her same thoughts and feelings. They are both avid artists and have expressed feelings of their childhood in many of their paintings. Lois also enjoys writing and illustrating children's stories for her three great-grand-children. She enjoys Florida life and her many trips to the Florida beaches with her sisters where she gets inspiration for her writings.

CPSIA information can be obtained
at www.ICGtesting.com
Printed in the USA
BVHW061322301018
531549BV00009B/19/P

9 781644 165102